The Real Housewiv[...]

The Dinner Party from HELL

A Coloring Book by DrunkDrawn

But I think it's generous of her to invite us all.
Give me a kiss you little sex monster.

Over at Camille's house, the party is about to begin...
Oh, I am so ready for a cocktail.
I waited until I got here.
I know. I got your text.
Allison Dubois
Medium / Camille's Friend

Camille said the more she drinks...

the more likely she is to have a feeling.

My new friends that you'll meet tonight.

And new friends that may end up being old frineds.

Patricia Arquette plays me.

I'm gonna have D.D. and Allison sit next to me.

See, I'm still young.

Camille's Confessional

The morally corrupt Faye Resnick.

And I have to say that I loved your spread.

Camille's Confessional
I mean, okay, we got into this conversation how I posed for Playboy too. But I was in my early 20s. I wasn't coming off of a big murder trial that my girlfriend was killed.
You know, that's just a whole different...I can't-- those kinds of people I don't understand and I don't want to associate with.
Those who live in glass houses should not throw stones.
And she threw a big boulder.

Kim's Confessional

And then Allison Dubois pulls out this electric cigarette. I think it's, like, a prop from some movie or something.

Kyle's Confessional

I'm thinking "that's Jack Nicholson from *The Shining.*"

Allison, I need to ask you something... Do you kind of feel like people that have passed are around?

If I'm at a dinner party with y'all, they got to take a second chair because you are the ones that I'm focused on.

But I head tap people too. So I pull thoughts. I can tap into somebody and be, like, "She has father issues. Her mother kept her mouth closed. Didn't stand up to the father. That's why she has mother issues. And the daddy issues. Daddy was like never there." So I start pulling that information.

I'm gonna have to watch you with these.

But it's a girls' night. So I'm off the clock.

She's off the clock. Maybe I should whip out my credit card.

Allison, can you do one person? Everybody is so excited about the fact that you are so gifted.

Don't tempt me. Really.

What does that mean: "Don't tempt me?"

As soon as the kids are bigger you'll have nothing in common.

Kim's Confessional

Ok. Here we go. I was waiting for Kyle to fly across the table.

Camille's Confessional

Kyle pushed for that reading. Allison already had a few drinks. Kyle pushed for it. I begged them not to go there because I think it's a personal reading.

That's me.

I feel also women are very catty to me.

They always will be.

By you saying that is saying that I'm not telling the truth.
Girlfriends tell each other what's really going on. Kyle tells me what's happening in her life. And if you were her good girlfriend you would know what's happening in her life.
So you're saying we're not good girlfriends because she didn't tell me what was happening?

My psychic ability tells me, "No."

If she needs my help, she will tell me. She doesn't rely on me. She can fight her on battles. If she can't fight her own battles and you have to be there, so be it but don't say I'm not there for Camille.

Faye, did you come here to defend Kyle? 'Cause the way you're talking sounds like she cued you in and you came to defend her.

Kim's Confessional

I don't do well with confrontation. And it was just coming from every direction.

All I know is there was an attack made on my friend in New York.

Camille's Confessional

Did I think it was a setup? Absolutely. Yeah. I thought Faye was there to be Kyle's wingman.

Camille, that's the way Faye sees it. Please we don't have to go ba—

How did I attack you?!

We're not allowed to talk to her about it cause she's now "Off the clock."

You're not hiring me. I'm a dinner guest. I was being polite. When y'all were irritating me, I appeased you. Be clear on that. I have books written on me and by me and had television shows based on my life.

So you can just, like, take a flying leap.

Walk. You've got two legs last time we checked.

Allison! Let me tell you something right now. All of this is unimportant to me. I have four beautiful children. Look how she turns her head like this. What are we in elementary school?

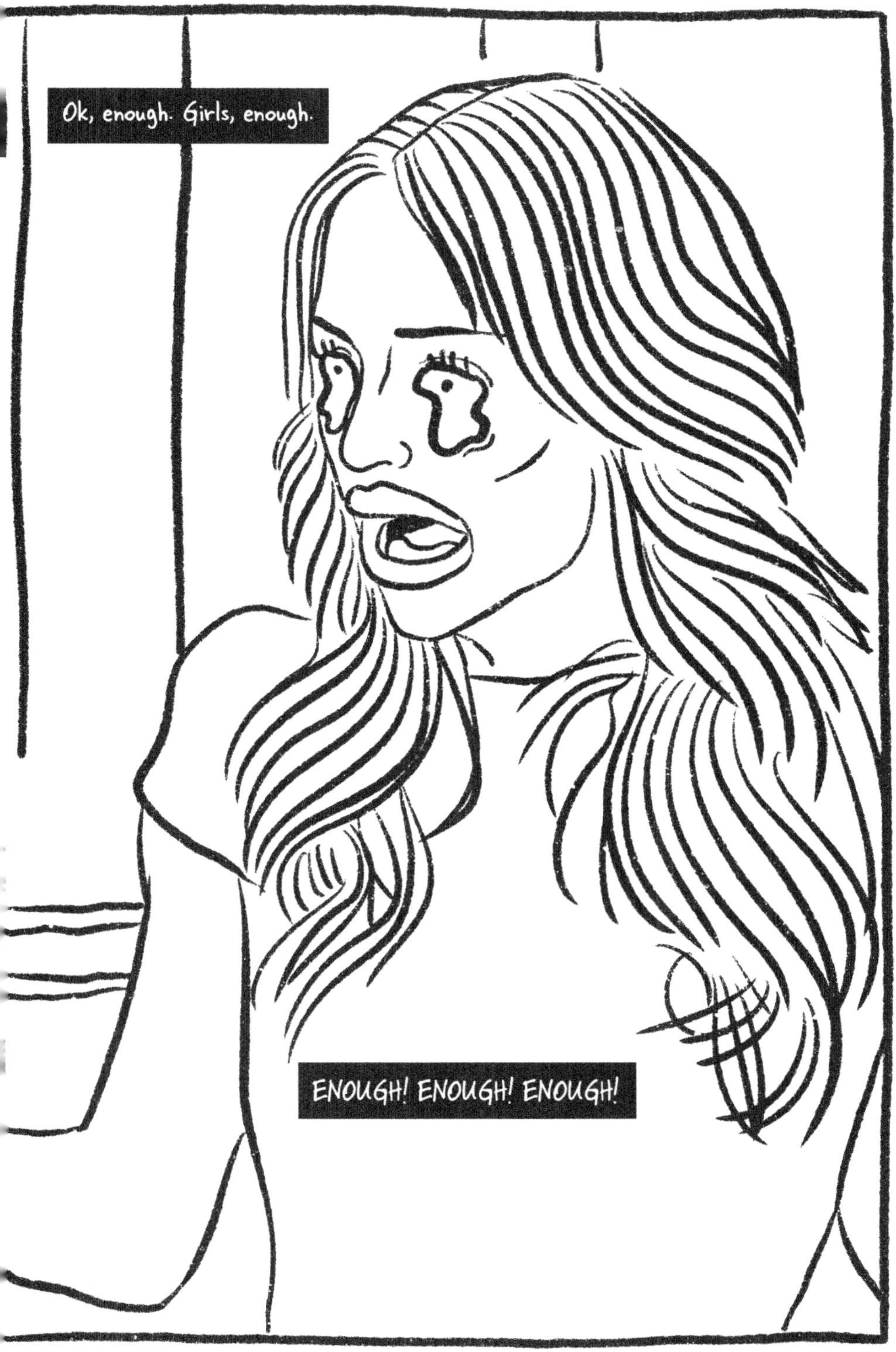
Ok, enough. Girls, enough.
ENOUGH! ENOUGH! ENOUGH!

Get up! These are not the ladies that we are. Enough.

My dad said, "Live life large and make no apologies for who you are." Fuck them.
I don't give a shit what she thinks about me. She can fuck off.

I can tell you when she will die and what will happen to her family. I love that about me.

Yeah, no, I think Kyle is morally bankrupt
I almost shoved this up her ass just to prove a point. Except I think she'd need a bigger one than this to even feel it. Oh, yeah, I went there.

Kyle is a conspirator. Know that.

Camille's Confessional

She came into my home and verbally assaulted me. Um, you know, fool me once, shame on— you know— how's it go?

We're the only sane people here. You and I need to stick together, ok?

We're gonna ride in one car and, Kim, you can take this car. I don't want to go out of the way. I just want to get home now.

Oh, that's good, all you ride together and talk about—

Kyle's an angry bitch. It's all she will be. Know that. She's unhappy with her life.

I think you're more on to her personal life with her husband than she wants to accept or she was even willing to accept it.

The End

Printed in Great Britain
by Amazon